Other Books By Michael J. Kiser:

4 Book Series called
"A Journey into the Spiritual Quest of Who We Are"

Book 1
~ The Reawakening ~
Book 2
~ Why Were They Called Gods? ~
Book 3
~The Knowledge that was once forbidden by some of the Ancient Beings ~
Book 4
~ The Quantum Leap into Consciousness ~

~~~

A Journey into the Spiritual Quest of Who We Are
Book 4
The Quantum Leap into Consciousness

By
Michael J. Kiser

Edited by
Heidi Erikson

DragonEye Publishing

A Journey into the Spiritual Quest of Who We Are: Book 4 -
The Quantum Leap into Consciousness
Copyright 2005
By Michael J. Kiser

All rights reserved, no Reproduction of any kind without the written permission from the Author and from the publisher.

Cover Design By Michael J. Kiser

Edited by Heidi Erikson

First Edition
First printing April 2005

ISBN 13: 978-0-9767832-4-4 (Paperback)
ISBN 13: 978-1-61500-078-4 (EPub Ebook)
ISBN 13: 978-1-61500-174-3 (PDF)

Publisher by Ancient Civilizations, an Imprint of DragonEye Publishing

www.DragonEyePublishers.com
email: Orders@DragonEyePublishers.com

DragonEye Publishing
753 Linden Place, Unit A
Elmira, NY 14901 USA

CONTENTS

1   Preface

    Chapter 1
5   The Creation of the Veils of Illusions
11 Breaking Away

    Chapter 2
15 The Start of a New Age

    Chapter 3
22 The Rite of Passage
30 The Next Step on the Ladder of Evolution
36 Becoming fully awaken Beings

    Chapter 4
42 Into the Unknown but Known
44 Understanding the Living Force
53 The One Path of many Journeys

    Chapter 5
59 The Departure of Some of the Previous Guardians
63 The Return of some Ancient Beings

    Chapter 6
78 Entering the Halls of Cosmic Creations
90 The Unseen World

    Chapter 7
93 The Arrival of new Guardians

    Chapter 8
99   Time Ends
101 Meeting with the Beings of Beings
103 A Message from the Ancient Beings of Beings

A Journey into the Spiritual Quest of Who We Are: Book 4
The Quantum Leap into Consciousness

Preface

Within is the fourth and final installment of the Kiazerian Journals, *A Journey into the Spiritual Quest of Who We Are.*

Herein Kiazer continues delving ever deeper, into the unknown, but also known. He continues removing the veils of illusion placed upon us around twelve thousand years ago. Understand this was done to keep us from learning the truth about ourselves.

I, the author, can only hope, that given all the knowledge Kiazer has shared with you throughout this entire series, you all will gain a much wider view of life and learn about who you really are. I hope that the insights that I have shared with you will help you in your reawakening, and I hope it helps to remove the veils of illusions. However, it is all up to each one of you to choose how you look at and use this knowledge of life that I am passing on to you throughout this series.

We all have to take this road in learning about who we are at some point in our lives. We all have those same questions about what life is all about and what it all means.

Finally, I hope that I had helped all of you to start your journey, in one form or another.

A Journey into the Spiritual Quest of Who We Are: Book 4
The Quantum Leap into Consciousness

A Journey into the Spiritual Quest of Who We Are: Book 4
The Quantum Leap into Consciousness

A Journey into the Spiritual Quest of Who We Are: Book 4
The Quantum Leap into Consciousness

Chapter 1

The Creation of the Veils of Illusions

*The human species really has no
idea who they really are,
since their consciousness has been asleep
for the past twelve thousand years!*

*It is time to, remove the veils of
illusions that we have all been living within!*

Kiazer talks to a group of people, he says "I have already shown you examples on how these beings have gone about creating fear and control. Now do you see the purpose for the veils that were created and placed upon you, for one reason and one reason alone?
 That reason was that these beings which had evolved before us thought they needed to create these veils of illusion to keep other beings from evolving in the knowledge of life. That knowledge is learning who we are as a spiritual being and learning what we are capable of becoming, through this

knowledge of life. So these older beings created stories to get the younger generation to believe in a certain way, which would keep us from asking and wondering of who we are in our life. So these beings created these stories which consist of telling the younger generations that they need to believe in a certain way based on this religious structure. This belief has been passed down from generation to generation with the fear of a god and that we all will be judged at the end of our life, based on how we lived our life based on this belief towards these so-called religions with these so-called gods."

As Kiazer walked around the group he mentions that "for some of those older beings of the past they did not want the younger generations evolving behind them, because some of these beings wanted to be in control of other beings/other civilizations that have not yet evolved like them. These stories are told repeatedly. In addition, no one can bring himself or herself to question the truth of these stories. This is mainly because most of the people in this day in age still live in fear of these beings that were playing these roles of these so-called gods thousands of years ago. Which I will remind all of you again that for the past six thousand years and as of now, no one has seen these so-called gods that people of today thought existed well over two thousand years ago. You will think at this day in age as this new millennium starts that people would have caught on by now, hearing the same stories repetitively and not witnessing a single god worldwide. You always hear people saying, "God says I must believe and act this way, or else." However, if you ask people did they see a god standing next to them when "he said" you must believe this way. People will say no, there was nobody next to me, but I heard a voice that told me that I must believe this way."

Kiazer said with sincerity and a louder voice, "Well if I heard a voice I would not call it god that's for sure. Even if this voice told me that he was god, I would ask him to prove it, because I know that all beings evolve at different times than others. It still does not make that being more of a god, than we as beings ourselves are."

The stories of these gods that were told well over ten thousand years ago still bring fear into people of today. This keeps the people from questioning the stories that they have heard that have been passed down through the ages. As long as you fear to look and question these stories, the longer it will be before you realize who you are. In addition, this will add to the time that you let these unseen so-called gods rule over your life with fear.

These stories were created as a veil to create the confusion which kept everyone at a stagnant evolution. People will continue telling these stories, of fear of these gods coming to judge them based on their religious beliefs, which were passed down. And these stories do change, with every time they

A Journey into the Spiritual Quest of Who We Are: Book 4
The Quantum Leap into Consciousness

are told. It was designed that way to keep all people confused in life and to bring the fear so they would not ask and wonder what life is about.

What a terrible way to live your life, and a controlled life at that point!

Why would anyone consider living a life under these conditions? This way of life takes away your life as the spiritual being that you are.

Why surrender your essence/your energy of life, to those beings? All they want is to control you and they are not even a god!

I have shown a lot to you through the previous three books. Some of these stories, of some of these beings, on their ways of controlling and bringing fear are to keep all of you from learning of the truth.

I am going to give you two more short examples of those stories of how these beings go about controlling you with these veils.

The first one is based on those Star Wars movies with the use of the Force – positive and negative energies. You have a being that is drawn to the negative energy and they use it as a way to control other beings in thinking since their power is stronger, (since it is of negativity). These beings go about making any civilization on any planet think that they have the power to destroy them if those civilizations do not obey this particular being. This being is of negative energy and creates fear to control a civilization into believing in this manner,

A Journey into the Spiritual Quest of Who We Are: Book 4
The Quantum Leap into Consciousness

so the civilizations go about obeying this being or they will be destroyed.

The second is from the stories of the movie Stargate and the TV series Stargate SG1 and their new series Stargate Atlantis. You have a being that had evolved to a point where it needs a host to continue to survive. This being is of a serpent – (snake), which needs a host – a human body or a humanoid body, so this being can continue on living for several hundreds of years or longer.

Now we have the mergence of two beings in one body. This evolved serpent being takes control of the body which it merged with, then they go about creating fear by the means of using this body to make other civilizations obey this being and make these civilizations think that this being is their gods.

Then you have civilizations fearing this being that is taking on this role of a god. Now you have these civilization fearing to question and afraid to learn of the truth. Then this being tells these civilizations that they need to believe this way and do not question their god, or they will be punished.

This all sounds too familiar to what is going on, on this planet with all the religions of these so-called beings that are playing these roles of gods and along with the governments, they all are creating this fear. These veils which were created, worked so well that you lived your entire life in fear of these stories of gods coming to Terra and judging you, if you went against these gods belief systems. For the past

A Journey into the Spiritual Quest of Who We Are: Book 4
The Quantum Leap into Consciousness

several thousands of years these veils worked so well that you forgot who you are.

With this insight you will understand how these beings are controlling you. You are allowing them to do so through your fears, and all these stories that you continue telling time after time.

How much longer are these stories of fear going to continue in your life?

Most of everyone today has lived their life by these stories. They only know about these stories because of their strong religious belief, which goes about telling them do not look at any other beliefs. In addition, their religions tell them do not question what is being told to you by their religions. People are also told that this is the only way of living your life and that there is no other way.

But there are a few people that know that there is more to life than what we are being told. We know this to be because we are not allowing ourselves to be controlled.

The old way of living is not needed any longer for us. We have lived this way far too long. Some people had that spark – a light within them that started that awakening and they realized these illusions were controlling them. Soon after they began to remove these veils, it started the reawakening of their spiritual self. They started this journey of a spiritual quest to learn who they were.

All these religious figures are not taking this lightly, because they are loosing their control over us. Which means that we are waking up and removing these veils of illusions and we are learning of this knowledge of life that we are part of, which they spent their entire life suppressing. As you begin to shed these veils, you will begin to see what the religions did not want you to see and to know the truth on what life is.

Breaking away

As you start your quest into your spiritual journey, you will begin to see how you were controlled by these stories of fear, which kept you stagnant from learning of the truth. You will be free to ask questions and to piece your search together on what life is really about, and you will learn about the many aspects that life has waiting for you.

As you begin this breaking away from this old way of life, it will be very confusing, since it is all new to you, in a way of speaking. You will find those stories which will conflict with the old way that you were brought up to believe in on how life was and how it is supposed to be as. There is a lot of knowledge out there, about life and who we are. You are not going to piece it all together, in a year or two, three. At least you have your foot in the doorway and you have the door open, to learn what has been kept from you all these years. Just reading

A Journey into the Spiritual Quest of Who We Are: Book 4
The Quantum Leap into Consciousness

this series shows you just that, this is your first step in that reawakening.

As you go down this road of learning about these aspects of life, it will feel as if this knowledge of life just keeps on flowing in like the faucet on a sink, turned on full and you cannot turn it off. It just keeps coming and coming.

Yeah, it will slow down enough so you can assess what has been presented to you. As soon as you have pieced together what you have just learned, it will start again with more knowledge about life. And once again you will have the time to assess what you had just learned.

You will start beginning to see how all the knowledge you were given falls into place, the things you were told to avoid so that you would not learn. I have brought some of this to light throughout this series. I have only presented a fraction of the pieces that are the main important part of my search to show where I am coming from with my knowledge of what is missing within this vast life of ours. I have only presented a very small tip of an iceberg, so to say, about the knowledge of life, beyond what we are brought up to believe in.

As you continue to delve ever deeper into the ancient myths of ancient forgotten knowledge of the ancient civilizations, you will also learn why those stories were changed from age to age. Now you can see why this confusion was brought about with today's belief systems.

A Journey into the Spiritual Quest of Who We Are: Book 4
The Quantum Leap into Consciousness

Now you begin to piece together what the religious figures know and tried to keep from you. Now you begin to realize the truth, behind the creation of these veils of illusions. As you learn more of the truth, you will find yourself not looking at religions in the same way, if you even look at them at all.

You are learning the truth of what life is about now. As you continue to unravel each story that you find which is older than the previous story, you will begin to see why these older stories were changed to the way they are today. These stories were changed to bring confusion about in life, to keep people from wanting to learn the knowledge of life, so people would not learn about the true aspects of their spiritual self and of who they are.

However, this is what you have done when you went out and started reawakening the knowledge of who you are.

This is what the religions were afraid might happen. They knew if you went out and learned the truth of who you are, that they would no longer have control of your life and that these beings had failed their so-called mission (keeping you from learning of the truth). As you continue down that path of spiritual reawakening, you become that spiritual being that we all are. And as long as you continue on this path these beings that want control over you will no longer have that control. For the past three thousand years all this knowledge about life was put aside by the religious figures. It is now being brought to light for all to learn the truth on what life is all about.

Claim the truth about what life is about, it is your right as the spiritual being you are.

Chapter 2

The Start of A New Age

Terra is about ready to make her quantum leap around 2020, where one Terrain world will stay in the 3rd dimension for those that need more time to make that transition of letting go of the old ways of life. The people of the 2nd world become the conscious beings and evolve from the original Terrain world and they will take that quantum leap into becoming that fully awakened conscious being.

Well I can say this, as I am writing now, which is December 2004, this particular event of having two Terrain worlds will not come to be as thought of in the past, this is due to the thought that this event of having two Terrain Worlds is no longer needed to be manifested.

Oh, we will have our quantum leap of consciousness!

For those that chose not to evolve spiritually, will leave Terra, for those that want war and to bring about war against other beings, they will not be part of Terra and they will be removed in one form or another.

The reason for the thought of having two Terra's in the past was mainly due to all the thought of negativity that most of the beings on your planet were creating within themselves and outside of themselves about life.

Since 1990 some people have been changing their thoughts of what is created around them. Plus the older generation of people of this negative thought of fear, war and destruction, have been leaving this planet. A new generation is being born, and these people are realizing its time for peace, a union is needed between all beings that are in existence on earth and amongst the universes.

After this transition is complete and we enter into our new age, you will feel as if the planet has become larger, but in fact the population will have dramatically been reduced to those that wish to evolve spiritually and peacefully and to become fully awakened conscious beings.

Let's hope that our past age of existence does not return to us at any time. Let's hope that we have learned our mistakes of the past eons.

Many people had come to fear this so called end times as told within the bibles.

Why so much fear towards an end?

It is all that control from all those belief systems that had created all that fear towards other beings of the past, the present, and the future. The belief

A Journey into the Spiritual Quest of Who We Are: Book 4
The Quantum Leap into Consciousness

systems created a negative view of life within most people about those battles of beings of good and evil, which will come to Terra to battle for the possession of this planet. The belief systems also created this fear within most people, that they need to live there life in a certain way to please their god(s) or their god(s) will judge them unworthy and that these god(s) will send the unworthy ones to the void or hell or whatever you want to call it. This is not so, as I mentioned and have shown you throughout this series.

This old pattern of energy is no longer part of the Terra's star system, as it prepares for a new beginning.

At the end of 1985, the Piscean age ended. It lasted for about 6 thousand years, and was known as the Dark Age, for its negative aspects such as war, turmoil, fear, and the controlling of the masses through deceptions such as the creation of the gods and devils theory, as has been described throughout this series.

1985 – 2000 was known as the transition period, the removing of the negative aspect (energy) of that previous age as described throughout this series.

As for this star system, it does not need this negative energy of any sort any longer. This planet has no need for this negative energy, which about 75 percent of her population had created for all to experience in one form or another during the Piscean Age. This planet no longer has any use of beings and/or people that desire to be negative and bring about destructiveness to those beings and/or people that are pure and positive. Those beings and people that are of negative will no longer be part of the earth or part of this universe, since everything is moving towards the positive energy.

It is at this point in time that everyone needs to restructure their views and thoughts and to let go of the previous age of thoughts of life. Let it all go, it is no longer a part of the New Age of Aquarius – The Age of Light.

Indeed 1985 was the end times, the end of an Age and a start of a new beginning, a new age.

The years 2000 – 2012 deal with the restructuring of the new energy for this new age. This new energy is of positive aspects, such as peace, harmony, and tranquility – all of humanity on Terra living as one. The end of 2012 begins our new age known as the Aquarian Age of Light.

This new age that we will enter in 2012 will bring forth the knowledge of life of who we are, in retrospect to those other beings which exist amongst the universes seen and unseen, as I presented throughout this series.

The knowledge of who we are will no longer be suppressed in this universe that we reside in.

As the earth and her people move forward in the evolution, so does the galaxy that we reside in, and so will the universe that our galaxy resides within. We all are making this transition, this leap into awakening this knowledge of realizing our potential as conscious beings.

As we enter our new age, we reawaken this knowledge that was once held by those Ancient of beings of ancient times that were on this planet earth, well over twenty thousand years ago.

This knowledge of life and the understanding of who we are is nothing new, we all go through these cycles of life where this knowledge lays dormant within us for periods. Until we emerge from our time of being asleep, to this awakening, this leap of consciousness of knowledge, the knowledge within all of us, within all beings that subsist amongst all the universes seen and unseen.

Most have been down this path, this road of changing of the ages, but not many of you remember, but all of that is changing now.

Like life the cycles of the ages are the one in the same. It is the process of Life.

Life and every age have one thing which is common to one another. That is that from life you have death, and from death you have life again, this is the cycles of the essence of life and of the ages, life after another one, age after another. One Age is of light (becoming awakened) and the other is of dark (being asleep). These cycles are always going from one to the other and back through the cycles over and over again, without ever ending.

A Journey into the Spiritual Quest of Who We Are: Book 4
The Quantum Leap into Consciousness

Each age goes from light to dark and back again, over and over again, the energy in each cycle is never the same. This is what we all are witnessing at this time, the end of an age and the start of a new age, the bringing fourth of this magnificent energy of light and peace to this new cycle of life.

You are all going to be part of the changes of course, and not everyone will survive these changes. For the ones that do survive, it will be a totally new place, a new planet for the future. In this cycle will come the revealing of the universal knowledge that's been kept hidden from many of you for about four thousand years. From this wisdom will come the everlasting peace that Terra, and her people have been expecting. Besides having peace, there will also be eternal life for those souls that choose free will, it's there for everyone.

Your new life within this era is a step up on the spiritual evolutionary ladder of the unlimited knowledge of the universal wisdom. In this era you will learn to develop into multi-dimensional beings, from this you will be leaving from your 3rd dimensional existence which is your 3rd dimensional solid body, to move into the 4th and 5th dimensional existence. Your soul and spirit will be able to exist outside of one another, at the same time simultaneously, coexisting within each others creations and being totally aware of your other self.

A Journey into the Spiritual Quest of Who We Are: Book 4
The Quantum Leap into Consciousness

This is the knowledge that has been dormant within your soul and spirit for thousands of years. The human race has always been trying to find the so-called missing link to evolution.

Well, it has been inside each and every one of you for thousands and thousands of years. It never left, not even for a second; you just did not want to take on the responsibilities. Do you see, what I am saying here?

This means going into the unknown, not knowing what might be coming your way, if it is for worse or for the better for your soul. But either way, if you look at it now, you will benefit from your own experiences of these events that are in front of you. Of course, everything you experience will be a step up on the evolutionary scale of existence going towards becoming a multidimensional being.

Then the New Age is really a point in time where the soul of every being has the chance to start the beginning of their new life, if it is in another cycle of life, or another dimension of existence. This is transpiring at this time for all to experience.

Chapter 3

The Rite Of Passage

During long forgotten times, many thousands upon thousands of years ago, these ancient civilizations, including those civilizations from not so long ago, all had knowledge and wisdom about the spiritual aspects of life and what life truly was about. These ancient civilizations' were more spiritually attuned to their higher selves. They were thousands of times more attuned than what we are today.

Those beings of the ancient times lived as one with all Terrain's and cherished each life that was upon Terra. All beings knew that they themselves and their world had a purpose in the cycle of life. Through this involvement, these beings were united as one by their spirituality and through the emergence with the Terrain's spirit. Being interconnected to each other and the planet itself, resulted in a merging that lifted the very essence of those beings to a higher spiritual understanding. Imagine what it was like to be aware and attuned, and living on a conscious planet. Terra, being conscious herself, taught those inhabitants about the cycles of life and about the spiritual growth of all life, including the planet, animals, plants, and even people. It was virtually the same for all types of beings.

This spiritual learning about life was not confined to the planet alone, because Terra travels through the Milky Way Galaxy and the beings that live on her gain knowledge about our solar system and the stars within this universe. The Terrains also learned that the universe is a consciousness living being and that the universe itself has life cycles involving the spiritual growth of creation. This is what the Terrain's spirit taught the inhabitants as they journey through the galaxy.

As Terra and her inhabitants journeyed through the universe, they crossed paths with other star systems that had other civilizations amongst them. Some of these beings within those other star systems were at greater or lesser degrees of spiritual evolution than the Terrain's were. In addition, some of those other civilizations were at the same level of spiritual growth as the beings of Terra.

After many generations, and as Terra continues her journey through the universe, the inhabitants began to understand more and more about their spirituality, life, and who they are. The inhabitants began to understand all aspects of many creations and their part in this cycle of life. The Terrains were realizing the essence of life, which is the essence of creation, and this realization alone has many aspects of growth within it. These beings were learning that the very nature of life consists of both physical and spiritual (energy) aspects. For instance, they learned about both the physical and spiritual essences of life, which can be physical or nonphysical (energy) and that neither can exist without its counterpart.

They knew that all these nonphysical (energy) bodies had their own physical structure, were beyond physical viewing. This takes into account that both astronomical bodies, such as planets, and other physical bodies, that are of humanoid form, are affected by being created out of nothing, and not always visible through physical perception.

Along with the physical aspects of all life, they also have other unseen energy, which is just beyond the physical perception, and although unseen, it can be felt. This energy (spirit) interacts with us in many ways and it shows us things in ways that we cannot perceive through our five senses, these ancient beings learned about their existence within both nonphysical energies of (soul – spirit), and physical matter. They are aware that both parts of themselves exist together as one unified being. Because if one form of their selves does not think that the other form exists, then the other part would not exist either. It is only through this acceptance of both forms, the physical (matter), and non-physical (spirit – soul /energy), exist through one another's thought (creation)- that each creates the other. Therefore, both beings exist together, but one cannot exist without the thought of their other, physical or nonphysical aspects of one's own self. It is in the thinking, which goes about creating each other at the same time in life.

These ancient beings understood the true meaning of the creation of life. That meaning is that the evolution process of the essence of the DNA that is spread across the multi universes. These nonphysical beings if they were of (the energy of souls / spirits) were able to watch life itself be created on a subatomic level as the planet evolved. This brought forth the creations of the many physical beings that that the planet had in mind at that particular time of the planets evolution. Then, after that creation was manifested into physical form, and after several millions of years, these ancient beings of energy and of spirit/soul, would eventually merge into those physical creations, bringing with them their knowledge of the vastness of the universes that these ancient beings had once came from to impart to those physical beings.

As these ancient beings of energy and those of souls/spirits started a new "co-existence" for all beings, they knew as they were in this physical form and living this life, they were involved in a new understanding of existence, which would be living as their energy existence or of their soul/spirit, within a physical form, until the next cycle where all will be separated as individuals once again.

A Journey into the Spiritual Quest of Who We Are: Book 4
The Quantum Leap into Consciousness

This is what is meant by cycles of creation between the physical and the beings of souls/spirits along with the ancient beings that had evolved into energy.

These beings began to realize that since they were creating their lives from incarnation to incarnation, it also meant that they must have been their own ancestors from time to time. Eventually, the knowledge that each life was their own, and they were recalling memories from several lives before, because they were aware that we go through living as spirit/soul or as an ancient being of energy, then merging within a physical life form and then the cycle starts over. Over and over again, experience after experience, which is what life is about, evolving physically and spiritually, into that being that we are. This is the same for all beings that are in existence and also for the planets and stars; they all go through this cycle of life, which is going from spirit (energy), into physical form and from physical into spirit (energy), lifetime after lifetime, ever so evolving from one form to the next.

These beings know this was the process of the cycles of life based on their knowledge, which they obtained when they came back into the physical world, from their existence as energy beings and as of a soul/spirit bringing the knowledge that they were finding what was left here from their previous lives. Such remembrances must be remnants from their previous lives, since they realized that they

A Journey into the Spiritual Quest of Who We Are: Book 4
The Quantum Leap into Consciousness

create their own material world, before they merged into a physical form again.

What these beings are remembering is past lives and what stage of evolution they were previously. They are able to recognize that they are evolving from what they were in the past to what they are at their present stage of evolution, not only physically and spiritually, but in some instances with their technology.

In other instances, at future lifetimes, these beings experience taking steps backwards in technology and lose knowledge about life and seemingly have to start all over again in learning about the true meaning of who we are.

During the past three thousand years to our present time, it seems that technology has been advancing by leaps and bounds. However, due to much knowledge of life being lost, the advanced technologies from some ancient civilizations have been hidden from us and it's as if we've been disconnected from the meaning of life altogether. We once understood the importance of cherishing all aspects of life. This used to include knowing that the human race lived as one and the understanding that we live on a conscious being, that is called planet Terra (Earth aka: Gaia).

Through these past two thousand years, we are repeating the same events unless we stop and realize what we are doing to ourselves as a human race. Look at what we have done to each other and to the planet that we all live on. At some point in the past, we all lived as one race on this conscious planet and we can do it again, if in the present time, enough of us become aware and enlightened about whom we really are.

Since we go through lifetime after lifetime on this planet, I can guarantee that we will be back on this conscious being in the not too distant future.

Sometime around twelve thousand years ago, our civilizations lost the knowledge of spirituality and we were brought up with the idea of a being that took on the role of a god. Additionally, that being was said to be male, it was claimed that he created everything, and we were told we should pray to him and recognize him as the almighty god.

Since then, all civilizations upon Terra were brought up with this concept of a being that is called god; a false notion is finally ending.

There is knowledge within all of us, but it has been shrouded in mysteries and concealed by the veils of illusions intended to keep us from learning about the true meaning of our essence and of life. This is mainly due to religions finding ways to control people and peoples' lives in many ways. Religions have been forced upon people, in part using crude behaviorism: with rewards and punishments. Though the use of fear, people can be manipulated. Religions threatened those who do not believe, with punishments such as eternal damnation (ie; burning in a hell fire for all of eternity). In contrast, rewards are offered to believers (eg; going to a supposedly blissful place called "heaven" for all of eternity).

However, for those experiencing the Rite of Passage, the path leads to learning the knowledge of life. These people are reawakening the essence that binds all life together. They are learning that they are all part of the essence of life and that we all create the existence that's around us, whether it's on Terra or it's among the stars.

As we enter into the new millennium 2,000 C.E. (Current Era), there are many individuals taking the Rite of Passage path. These people are realizing and understanding the knowledge of life and are starting to gain a different view of life. People of this new generation know that there is more to life than what they have been told through the years. As this knowledge from certain ancient civilizations is reawakened, the spiritual people along with the Shamans are reminding us that we, and the planet, are all connected to each other through what is called the essence. This essence is "the life force/energy, and it is not a, being (i.e. god), but it is energy which binds all life together within the universes, whether seen or unseen."

This is what this Rite of Passage is about, realizing that all those beings of the past, which were us going through this cycle lifetime after lifetime, are going to become like the spiritually advanced "ancients" in the future.

A Journey into the Spiritual Quest of Who We Are: Book 4
The Quantum Leap into Consciousness

The Next Step on the Ladder of Evolution

For those that have chosen this period, to take the next step on the ladder of evolution, it will lead to a leap of evolution in consciousness. During this quantum leap in conscious evolution, you will merge into the very essence of life itself. You will be experiencing what will feel like a jolt of electrical current through both of your bodies, the physical as well as the spirit (energy). This jolt is the process of the knowledge of the essence of life. This knowledge is separate from what you had thought life was really about, this is the true knowledge of life, and you already have a glimpse of it throughout this series. This knowledge is remembered through that rite of passage, the path that you started. Through free will of choice, a decision to let go of false ideologies, you can reawaken the knowledge that is rightfully yours.

Without realizing it, we have all been on this ladder of evolution from the very beginning of time, and we have already started that next step in the process, which is part of that cosmic ladder of evolution.

It is through this knowledge, which is a means to an end along with your own insight into the questions of life and what life is all about, that you open up to knowledge within yourself. This is only the beginning of what is to come for those that are ready for it. However, for the other people that choose not to open their minds at this time, they will not be prepared to make this leap. Nevertheless, for you, this time has come. You took the initiative, and by taking a step forward beyond the fear, you are seeking answers from within yourself.

You are becoming that being, who no longer looks outside themselves and to religions to find answers. You are going beyond that wall, which many do not want to take down, and adventuring further.

As you reawaken to this knowledge of life, you will become teachers to those people who were once like you at some point. Those people who still fear what is beyond the unknown – beyond the unseen, beyond the unexplained – and beyond the beyond.

What is this next step of consciousness about?

What can be said about our next step of evolution?

What haven't I already presented throughout this series?

I hope all of you were taking notes!

Because, I do not think there is much more to talk about. I do believe that we brought all the knowledge to light about this next step of consciousness.

A Journey into the Spiritual Quest of Who We Are: Book 4
The Quantum Leap into Consciousness

Well, you came this far in learning about the knowledge of life, and you are here once again to learn right? So why stop?

Ok, I see you choose to continue on, because you are still here.

Let's see what we can bring to light other than what we already presented to you.

This calls for all to participate in this exercise.

Take a moment; let's go outside and sit on the ground, now take a deep breath, and let it out, another deep breath and out, again, another deeper breath. Very good relax.

Clear your mind of all thoughts. Ok, are we ready? Good, let's begin.

The first and only question that I want all of you to ask is, "What is this next step of consciousness?"

Now look around you, look at the ground that you're sitting on…

Listen to what you hear around you…

Look at the sky, which is above you – if you are outside at night, look at the night sky with the stars…

Now close your eyes and sense what you feel, that which you cannot see…

Now, what you have learned about the knowledge of life?

What did you sense and feel during that moment?

A Journey into the Spiritual Quest of Who We Are: Book 4
The Quantum Leap into Consciousness

Do not look for my answers on the next page because they are not there. They are throughout the entire series.
It is a process...

Your answers please...
(You can use a separate sheet of paper.)

....

....

Now look at the people you see out and about. What do you feel and sense?

....

....

Look at the animals around you as well.
What do you feel and sense about them?

....

....

A Journey into the Spiritual Quest of Who We Are: Book 4
The Quantum Leap into Consciousness

Next, in your mind, unless you can physically, let's journey to see the whales and dolphins.
What do you feel and sense about them?

....

....

This time go deep within yourself, into your very "soul/essence".
What do you feel?

....

....

How about feeling the planet earth?
What do you feel within her energy?

....

....

Now look at the stars in the night sky.
What do you feel?

....

....

A Journey into the Spiritual Quest of Who We Are: Book 4
The Quantum Leap into Consciousness

This is what the next step of our Quantum leap of consciousness is all about, people looking, feeling, understanding, and going beyond the beyond. Beyond the physical realms and tangible objects that are all around us.

As we venture into this next step, realize, and become what is around you. Learn what life is and what is truly waiting for you.

We must show the way to those who fear the unknown and the unseen aspects of life. Consider that at some point in ones life, some of us have feared the unknown and the unseen.

Remember, not all beings and people take this step of evolution at the same time. Therefore those of you who do take this step forward, please be prepared to teach those that have not taken this step forward for whatever reasons they have. Be patient with them and help them understand. Let them know that you were once where they are now and that they can move to the next step where you are at this point. It's important that you also remind them everyone is always moving onto the next step of life. It's just a matter of when. Remember the ladder that we all are on never ends because there is always something and/or someone who is beyond where you are. It's an ongoing path of evolution in consciousness.

This is what our next step on the ladder of evolution is all, it's not just that one-step per lifetime that people think it is. Every step is presented to all of us during every lifetime it is how many steps each of us are willing to take in our current lifetime. We are not limited to just taking one step. How many steps you take on this ladder of life is up to you and you alone.

Nevertheless, you also need to remember what you have learned is there for all to learn and become what you have became. You also need to teach those who have not learned what you have learned, so they too may become as you are.

Becoming fully Awaken Beings

As you begin taking this next step into the evolution of consciousness, there are several steps within this one step.

The first step was the exercise a couple pages back, that I had you do. That exercise was for you to see if you could feel the energy force within all things. This energy force is both inside and outside of you. It is intended to make initial contact with the energy force that binds all life together. This energy force is not a being that you call god, it is merely energy of all living beings no matter if they are human, animal, other beings, plants, rocks, the planets, or the stars. This energy force is even amidst the open space between the universes. This life force, this energy is everywhere and everything.

The second step within this consciousness is where you release any doubts that you are not worthy of becoming a reawakened being that's within yourself, because that is who you really are. If you've been told you could not become that being until a much later time, you must come to terms with yourself and let your inner self (your soul/essence) bring its consciousness forth. This will help you overcome any physical limitation that has been placed on the physical understanding of the physical and the inner self.

How does one take this step?

If you have any doubts that you are not ready or worthy, release them and say that you are ready to become awakened and that you want to become the being that is within you.

It will not happen if you do not want it to. You must want this to be, it is the only way for this to be brought forth. It must be of your own free will and wanting this to be. You must realize that you have accomplished all that you have set out to do in your existing incarnation, and that you are ready to move on to becoming that being you want to be. If you think that you have not accomplished what you set out to do, then you will not be able to move forward. Not until you realize that you have accomplished

A Journey into the Spiritual Quest of Who We Are: Book 4
The Quantum Leap into Consciousness

what you have set to do. That is necessary before you can become who you truly are.

If you chose not to become that being that's within you, you will stay where you are now and won't evolve into what you truly are. Once you accept who you are within yourself, don't continue to look outside yourself for whom you are, or else the being within you will not come forth. First, you have to realize that you have been looking outside yourself and shift your focus to your true inner self that's always been who you are. Then, you will become an awakened being amongst the many!

All that has been mentioned above is about becoming reawakened beings while in the physical form.

'You can also achieve becoming that awakened being at the time of passing from this life to the next life. However, it is the same as the physical except nothing changes. It's just that you decided to continue your work on the other planes of existence.

On the other hand, you may choose to leave this life and come back into this physical life as a fully awakened being. All this can be achieved at this time due to the New Age we are now entering. In this New Age the knowledge of our fully awakened consciousness will be commonly known due to the many fully awaken beings whom are amongst you at this point. This is our next step in awakening the knowledge within about who we are.

A Journey into the Spiritual Quest of Who We Are: Book 4
The Quantum Leap into Consciousness

There is no longer a need for these veils of illusion from the past ages because we are moving beyond this world of limitations.

We are now becoming awakened beings and becoming that being which we all have been looking outside of ourselves for, for the past twelve thousand years. We are now awakening the same knowledge that all the Ascended masters and the Spiritual teachers of the past were trying to teach us, for the past seven thousand years, of who we are, as a conscious being. It is within this time that we are now able to take this step into becoming fully awakened beings, and realizing whom we are.

As we begin to become the beings that we are, as we enter into our new cycle of life, we are also at the same awakening point of those ancient beings were at one-hundred thousand years ago during their existence and their spiritual awakening of learning of who they were as conscious beings. They too came to the realization that they were the one that they too were looking outside of themselves to find, as being the one, and the only one being. These ancient beings also finally came to the acceptance that they were there own creator and no one else was.

They realized that this one being, did not exist, that it really was themselves being separated from there own inner selves and that all beings are there own one being and that each of us are, our own creator of our own life, and that no one else has power over us or that creates another one life.

This is the knowledge that is becoming reawakened within all of us, for those that are ready for this knowledge of who we are.

This is the true knowledge that all those Spiritual teachers were teaching to us, all those thousands of years ago, but the beliefs systems of that time did not allow this to happen, as I mentioned throughout this series.

Now is the time for all that knowledge to come forth and to be with us, at the new beginning that is in front of us.

That knowledge of those Spiritual Beings which was teaching us, that there was no need to look outside of oneself to know who we were, as the beliefs systems were teaching people. This belief system had gone and separated you from that knowledge and controlled all with the fear, to anyone which to seek this knowledge of inner knowing, the looking within ones inner self as this one being, was corrupt and went against gods will and will be destroyed, as I mentioned throughout this series.

This knowledge is nothing new to any of us, since the past is of the future and the future is of the present.

What was of the past is also coming to us now; it is the continuing endless cycles of life. It's like the physical cycles of life, you are born and then you die, and born again, so on and so on, as life goes on, never ending.

This is also true for the knowledge within us.

We go through periods of time which are of light (awakening), to the time of dark (being asleep), and back into the light, these cycles repeat themselves over and over again. But through these periods of the ages, they are thousands of years at a time; we are awakening and becoming who we are. We are that one being that we have been looking outside of ourselves to find. Nevertheless, we cannot find that one being, because we are that one being, which we have all been looking for.

Chapter 4

Into the Unknown... But Known

    The knowledge of the past will again, be the knowledge of the future in the present.
    What do all the cultures of the past, present, and the future have in common?
    All these cultures that were part of the earth of the past ages, along with the present age, tell us about our existence, and of our future.
The unknown is only unknown, to the one that does not, want to journey to the known. As I mentioned earlier in Book 3, this is your rite of passage, to know of this knowledge within you, to know the unknown. It is your right to walk beyond where others do not wish to journey because they feel that they do not have that right to go into the unknown and to know what is before them, for their own reasons.
    Like all ancient beings of the many cultures of the past, you too are walking into the unknown to the known and awakening the same knowledge that the ancient beings also awoke within themselves. But for you those that are reading this series, you

have started that journey into the unknown, to know what only seemed to be unknown.

The unknown is really something that is not known at the moment, a place in our existence of the future for instance. Many people are uncertain of their future because they say it is unknown and not for us to know about.

Well they are wrong!

As I mentioned this is our rite of passage. This knowledge of walking beyond and knowing the unknown and making it known is part of the ladder of evolution of becoming conscious beings.

As you journey into the unknown it becomes your known knowledge. As you learn of this knowledge of evolution, you begin to wonder what is beyond you, but you know from previous experiences that you can learn what is unknown by just journeying to a place beyond the present. The unknown becomes known when you merge into the unknown and learn about the knowledge, which was beyond where you were at in the past.

There were many ancient beings from ancient pre-civilizations that journeyed to the unknown to learn about what was beyond the beyond and to learn from other ancient beings. There are always other beings above us, which can teach us about what is unknown. We can also come across beings that do not want us to learn of what is beyond. The same goes for the beings that are below us, which have not learned what we have learned.

A Journey into the Spiritual Quest of Who We Are: Book 4
The Quantum Leap into Consciousness

I would like to take a moment and bring forth an example of knowledge from the unknown to the known, out how religions want to control us. This is based on a five thousand years old belief system.

This is an excerpt from the Journey of Self – discovery – By His Divine Grace, A. C. Bhaktivedanta Swami Prabhupada, pgs. 10-14 *(the italics are mine)*

Understanding the living Force

The International Society for Krishna consciousness is a movement aiming at the spiritual reorientation of mankind through the simple process of chanting the holy names of god. The human life is meant for ending the miseries of material existence. Our present – day society is trying to end these miseries by material progress. However, it is visible to all that in spite of extensive material progress, human society is not peaceful.

The reason is that the human being is essentially a spirit soul. It is the spirit soul that is the background of the development of the material body. However the materialistic scientists may deny the spiritual existence in the background of the living force, there is no better understanding than accepting this living force as ultimately the spirit soul within the body.

A Journey into the Spiritual Quest of Who We Are: Book 4
The Quantum Leap into Consciousness

The body is changing – from one form to another – but spirit soul which existing externally, which changes. This fact we can experience even in our own life. Since the beginning of our material body in the womb of our mother, our body has been changing from one shape to another at every second and at every minute. This process is generally known as "growth" but actually it is a change of body.

On this earth, we see change of the day and night and change of season. The more primitive mentality attributes this phenomenon to changes occurring in the Sun.

For example, in the winter primitive people think the sun is getting weaker, and at night, they presume, sometimes, that the sun is dead. With more advanced knowledge we see that the sun is not changing at all in this way. Seasonal and diurnal changes are attributed to the changes of the relative positions of the earth to the sun.

Similarly, we experience bodily changes: from embryo to child to youth to maturity to old age to death. The less intelligent mentality presumes that after death the spirit soul's existence is forever finished, just as primitive tribes believe that the sun dies at sunset. Actually, however, the sun is rising in another part of the world.

(But we know that the sun does not move, it is the planets that are rotating).

Similarly, the soul is accepting another type of body. When the body gets old like an old garment and is no longer usable, the soul accepts another body, just as we accept a new suit of clothes. Modern civilization is practically unaware of this truth.

People do not care about the constitutional position of the soul. *(This is due to belief systems, which are not allowing people to know the real truth).* There are different departments of knowledge in different universities and many technological institutions, all to study and understand the subtle laws of material nature, and there are medical research laboratories to study the physiological condition of the material body, but there is no institution to study the constitutional position of the soul. This is the greatest drawback of materialistic civilization, which is simply an external manifestation of the soul.

People are enamored of the glittering manifestation of the cosmic body or the individual body, but they do not try to understand the basic principle of this glittering situation. The body looks very beautiful, working with full energy and exhibiting great traits to talent and wonderful brainwork. But as soon as the soul is away from the body, this entire glittering situation of the body becomes useless. Even the great scientists who have offered many wonderful scientific contributions have been unable to trace out the personal self, which is the cause of such wonderful discoveries.

The krsna consciousness movement, therefore, is basically trying to teach this science of the soul, not in any dogmatic way, but through complete scientific and philosophical understanding. In the background of this body you can find the soul, whose presence is perceivable by dint of consciousness. Similarly, in the universal body of the cosmic manifestation, one can perceive the presence of the super soul and super consciousness.

The absolute Truth is systematically explained in the Vedanta sutra (generally known as the Vedanta philosophy), which in turn is elaborately explained by the Srimad – Bhagavatam, a commentary by the same author. The Bhagavatam – gita is the preliminary study of the Srimad - Bhagavatam for understanding the constitutional position of the supreme lord, or the absolute truth.

An individual soul is understood in three aspects: first as the consciousness pervading the entire body, then as the spirit soul within the heart, and ultimately as a person. Similarly, the absolute truth is first realized as impersonal Brahman, then as localized super soul (Paramatma), and at the end as the supreme personality of godhead, krsna. Krsna is all – inclusive. Or in other words, krsna is simultaneously Brahman, Paramatma, and the personality of godhead, just as every one of us is simultaneously consciousness, soul, and person.

The individual person and the supreme person are qualitatively one but qualitatively different. Just like the drop of seawater and the vast mass of seawater – both are qualitatively one. The chemical composition of the drop of seawater and that of the mass of seawater are one and the same. But the quantity of salt and other minerals in the whole sea is many, many times greater than the quantity of salt and other minerals contained in the drop of seawater.

The krsna consciousness movement upholds the individuality of the soul and the supreme soul. From the Vedic Upanishads we can understand that both the supreme person, or god, and the individual person are eternal living entities. The different is that the supreme living entities, or supreme person, maintains all the innumerable other living entities. *(This is what the religions want us to believe, that we are separated and that some other being controls us).* In the Christian way of understanding, the same principle is admitted, because in the bible it is taught that the contingent entities should pray to the supreme father so that He may supply means of maintenance are given pardon for their sinful activities.

So it is understood from every source of scriptural injunction that the supreme lord, or krsna, is the maintainer of the contingent living entity and that it is the duty of the contingent entity to feel obliged to the supreme lord. Thus is the whole background of religious principle. Without these acknowledgements there is chaos, as we find in our daily experience at the present moment.

The chaos is created by the religions to keep us from realizing that all of us are this god. Just because a particular being is further up on the ladder of evolution than we are, doesn't make that being any more of a god than we are. It's religions that do not want us to realize those aspects.)

This is the knowledge that we are reawakening within all of us, as we enter this New Age.

Everyone is trying to become the supreme lord, socially, politically, or individually. Therefore there is competition for this false lordship, and there is chaos all over the world individually, nationally, socially, and collectively. The krsna consciousness movement is trying to establish the supremacy of the absolute personality of godhead. One who has attained a human body and intelligence is meant for this understanding, because this consciousness makes his life successful.

The religions do not want the individual to realize who they are because when the individuals learn that every one of us is this god, then these religions will no longer have control over us, as they have for the past twelve thousand years. The only chaos is that the religions are losing their control and they will go to any extent to stay in control of us.

A Journey into the Spiritual Quest of Who We Are: Book 4
The Quantum Leap into Consciousness

This krsna consciousness movement is not a new introduction by mental speculators. Actually, this movement was started by krsna Himself. On the battlefields of Kuruksetra, at least five thousand years ago, the movement was presented by krsna in the Bhagavad – Gita. From Bhagavad – Gita we can also understand that he had spoken this system of consciousness long, long before – at least 120,000,000 years ago – when he had imparted it to the sun – god, Vivasvan.

So this movement is not at all new. It is coming down in discipline succession from all the great leaders of India's Vedic civilization, including Sankaracarya, Ramanujacarya, Madhvacarya,
Vishnu Svami, Nimbarka and lately, about 480 years ago, lord Cartanya. The discipline system is still being followed today. This Bhagavad –Gita is also very widely used in all part of the world by great scholars, philosophers, and religionists. But in most cases the principles are not followed as they are. The krsna consciousness movement presents the principles of the Bhagavad – Gita as they are – without any misinterpretation.

From the Bhagavad – Gita can understand five main principles, namely god, the living entity, the material and spiritual nature, time and activities. Out of these five items, god, the living entity, nature (material or spiritual), and time are eternal. But activities are not eternal.

A Journey into the Spiritual Quest of Who We Are: Book 4
The Quantum Leap into Consciousness

Activities in the material nature are different from activities in the spiritual nature. Through the spirit soul is eternal (as we have explained); activities performed under the influence of the material nature are temporary. The krsna consciousness movement aims at placing the spirit soul in his eternal activities. We can practice eternal activities even when we are materially engaged to act spiritually simply requires direction, but it is possible, under the prescribed rules and regulations.

As I have mentioned throughout this series, this is the control of the religions, by keeping all of you stagnant it will keep all of you from learning the truth of who we are. These religions go about placing rules and regulations, and saying that you can only go to a certain point and you cannot look and know beyond what they want you to know.

The krsna consciousness movement teaches these spiritual activities, and if one is trained in such spiritual activities, one is transferred to the spiritual world, of which we get ample evidence from the Vedic literatures, including the Bhagavad – Gita. The spiritually trained person can be transferred to the spiritual world easily – by change of consciousness.

One does not need to be trained to enter this spiritual world. The spiritual world is all around us; it is within us, all we need to do is look within and see that spiritual world; we all merge into this spiritual world when we meditate and when we enter into that sleep state.

Consciousness is always present, because it is the symptom of the living spirit soul, but at the present moment our consciousness is materially contaminated. For instance, water pouring down from a cloud is pure, but as soon as the water comes in touch with the ground it becomes muddy – immediately. Yet if we filter the same water, the original clearness can be regained. Similarly, krsna consciousness is the process of clearing our consciousness and as soon as our consciousness is clear and pure eternal life of knowledge and bliss. This is what we are hankering for in this material world, but we are being frustrated at every step on account of material contamination. Therefore, the leaders of human society should take this krsna consciousness movement very seriously.

End of Excerpt

This is what the religions want us to continue in believing in, so that we give up our rite of passage of realizing and becoming our own god. That old way of believing, that there is one god and that he is in control of us, is coming to an end, very, very quickly, as we make this transition into our New Age.

A Journey into the Spiritual Quest of Who We Are: Book 4
The Quantum Leap into Consciousness

What knowledge does the unknown brings to us?

As we journey into the unknown it will become known. We learn the knowledge of life; we reawaken this knowledge of our consciousness, our essence, and our connection to the energy life force, which binds all life together. We learn that we create our existence through this awakening consciousness. We are learning that our future is being created through this energy force – this essence of life, through our own thoughts as we go about wondering about our future.

As we continue to journey to that which is considered our future or that is beyond us, eventually it becomes our present and again we create what is beyond us again that unknowing of the future, so on and so on, never ending cycle of creating the unknown, the creating of your future.

This is the knowledge that the unknown brings to us as conscious beings, which is, that we create our future in the past to experience in the present.

The one Path of Many Journey's

We all find ourselves on that one path of looking outside of ourselves to find and to believe in one being, that was out there, that we were told not to look within to find, because it was not within us, it was outside of us, which was a being that created us in his image. We journeyed down that path for eons, during those many ages that brought us to this time that is now. We have come to realize that there is more than we were led to believe about our existence, of our life, and of who we are. As we begin our next journey, we no longer have these veils of the past, which kept us from all the knowledge of our existence, the knowledge of who we are, and the knowledge of what is to come. We are now finally able to see all that is around us, due to what is called the removal of the walls or the opening of the doorways, which have been closed to us for the past twelve thousand years.

Now that we are able to journey into that unknown and make it the known, we have come to the realization of those many journeys which await us as we start down this new path. This journey is not for a select few; this journey is a journey for all, we all exist together within the creation that we all created for our existence.

What does life offer to us now that these walls are gone, and the doorways are all open for all of us to experience the unlimited knowledge? This knowledge was once unknown to us during the dark ages. The dark ages dealt with being asleep and have come to a close, to bring forth the age of awakening of the knowledge within.

What will it be like when we finally become that conscious being, as we all realize that we are the creators of our existence? We put that burden upon a

A Journey into the Spiritual Quest of Who We Are: Book 4
The Quantum Leap into Consciousness

being that has no responsibility for our creation; this burden of our creation is our own burden and no one else's. This is all of our creation within and around all of us and we all have to take the responsibility for it. If there is something in your creation that you do not want in your creation any longer, just simply remove it out of your experience and make your experience in this creation the way you want it to become. Some might even say that they did not create this war – destruction.

Remember this is of the old ways, which is no longer part of this New Age that we are entering into, because many of us are realizing that we do not need this any more so it is becoming something of the past. Remember, what one creates in their creation another one might experience your creation somewhere along their creation as well, since there is one path and many on these journeys within this path. This is where we have other people and other beings come into our creation.

A Journey into the Spiritual Quest of Who We Are: Book 4
The Quantum Leap into Consciousness

Imagine one path and off this path you have millions of paths to journey within.
It might look something like this!

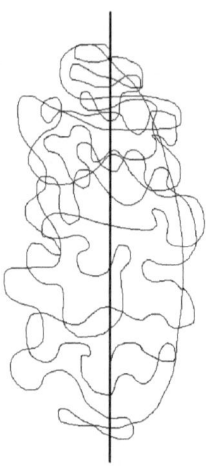

All will come to experience the awe, the wonder, the unknown of what is around the bend on the next path of this journey, which is unfolding before you. As if you were the creator of what is to come. Which this is true, you are creating what is waiting for you, since this path, this journey is yours and yours alone. You are your own creator of your life and your experiences within yourself; this is what you are creating outside of yourself, as well to experience as your creation.

A Journey into the Spiritual Quest of Who We Are: Book 4
The Quantum Leap into Consciousness

This massive creation that we all are journeying within is not created by any one being. This massive creation which we all are part of is created by all of the beings of the past and of the future, which is created in the present, the now, which is of all the thoughts that are projected out from all beings which exist within the universes seen and unseen. I talked about the process of thought in Books 1 and 3, about how thought is a very powerful thing to all beings and which includes the life force, the energy which makes the suns, the energy which brings all these planets into manifestations from energy into the physical form, and all these suns which come together to create these galaxies and all those galaxies into creating universes that create other universes among universes.

We must remember as we traverse on our journey, there are others that are on their creation as well. As all merges into each other's creation you have to understand that each of you are creating each other into your own creation simultaneously without realizing it in a way, since each of you is the creator of your own creation.

This new journey that we are embarking on is about us being the creators of our own creation, that is unfolding in front of us all, as we go forward into what might be the unknown, but it is also the known, since we have already thought what this unknown might be. See, the unknown is really something that you already created in the past, for your future. So, now your future is here now, from your past thoughts, of the unknown, which the unknown is really your own creation of the past becoming created in the future, which that future, is now here for you to experience what you had created in the past for yourself for the future.

So when people say that they do not know what is in store for them in the future, they are misleading you and themselves. We all know what is in store for us in the future, since we all create our future in the past to be experienced in the future, which becomes our present, our now.

Chapter 5

The departure of
Some of the Previous Guardians

In the 3rd Book of this series I talked a little about the Ancient Guardians of Terra of the past.

These guardians were of many origins, to name a few not in any particular order, there were those of: Vishnu's – Avatars – Wizards – Cetaceans as of the Whales – Dolphins – the Nefilem – the Elves and many more. Some guardians that we all have read about within the myths and tails of the past ages are all indeed true, and were all a part of the Guardians of Terra, many, many eons ago.

But there is one group out of the many of the past that has stayed around and watched over all of the Earths happenings. Even at this moment they are among us, watching and monitoring the progress of our, "human Quantum leap of consciousness," as the beings of consciousness that we are.

This group of guardians has decided on its own to stay and monitor the progress of Terra as the conscious being that she is. Terra is a host to all

A Journey into the Spiritual Quest of Who We Are: Book 4
The Quantum Leap into Consciousness

those beings that will inhabit Terra through her many ages and cycles.

    This one group of guardians is always seen by us, the humans on the earth and we do not fear them. We see these guardians among us in our surroundings when we have that moment to see them, since the people have been around these guardians for thousands of years. We the people had grown to love these magnificent beings, even though most of us had no idea about them being the guardians of this earth, other than very few of us that knew they were the guardians.
    For those of you that said the cetaceans, whales, and dolphins are the guardians you are correct!

Yes, these whales and dolphins are the guardians and they have been keeping tabs on all that has been transpiring on this planet, along with how the human species has been evolving, and how we treat other beings that are upon Terra. When I say "how we treat other beings," that goes for all species on the earth, it goes for the human species because we are no different than any other life that is on this earth. This earth is also a living conscious being even though most people have no concept of the earth as being a conscious being. This also goes for how we treat other beings that come to the earth from other star systems which are far beyond ours. These Cetacean guardians have been recording all that has been transpiring on Terra for eons. They have done their part in balancing the energies of their positive energy on Terra, despite all the negativity that most of our species has been creating upon the planet and amongst the civilizations of humans that are spread across the entire world and the destruction that we are doing to our own species

Yes, this is all recorded by these guardians, which are among you, and not by a being, "saying he is your god," but by all beings of consciousness, which are not any different than you, other than they already became beings of consciousness eons ago. This is what some of us, the human beings, are going through, this transition and realizing who we are and our responsibility of becoming the conscious beings that we are.

A Journey into the Spiritual Quest of Who We Are: Book 4
The Quantum Leap into Consciousness

Back in 1992 – 1993, there were few dolphins and whales that beached themselves, and people that were witnessing these events as they were happening tried to help these beings back into the water. But those beings of those whales and dolphins choose not to return to the water because, their time came and they wanted to leave this plain of existence of this 3rd dimension. They wanted to leave in this fashion of having those people showing compassion to them and to be there for their ascension as they entered the 4th and 5th dimensions of existence. They contribute their existence in the 3rd dimension as these guardians. These beings are still continuing to contribute their energy and knowledge from the 4th and 5th dimension plains of existence; it was just that these beings decided to continue their work in a different way, to assist this new energy that is coming to the earth at this point in time.

We all have to remember that the Cetaceans beings are the oldest beings of Terra, which we all are comfortable seeing in our everyday life. Moreover, at the same time we have to come to the realization that these beings are the guardians, as well they help balance the earth of most people's thoughts of negativity. These guardians are more capable of balancing the energy, since they were doing this for many eons past.

A Journey into the Spiritual Quest of Who We Are: Book 4
The Quantum Leap into Consciousness

Now comes the time that most of these Cetacean beings will be leaving this plain of existence. But I assure you, a few will stay a little bit longer on their decision alone. But only if we, the human beings, can show respect to all beings that exist on the earth, and too these other beings that are not of this earth, when that time comes for that mass involvement with these other beings, which are from your universe and from universes beyond yours.

Some of you might say, "Well that has been going on for awhile."

Well you are right! However, on a very limited involvement though. As you know, some off world beings have been involved within the government and the religions, as I have presented throughout this whole series. But all that is going to be changing, and this involvement will be on a global scale with other worldly beings, as we learn this knowledge of becoming conscious beings within this vast universe that we all are part of.

The Return of some Ancient Beings

Within all of the previous 3 books, I talked some about the Ancient Guardians/Watchers that were among the civilizations of ancient times. These beings are returning, as we are entering into our new age, a new beginning, we will be seeing some of those ancient beings returning to our star system and to our planet. These ancient beings have been watching over us from afar and they have been monitoring our star system for thousands and thousands of years, with very little interaction with us from time to time over the course of thousands of years. For those that were and still are less fortunate to have these interactions with those ancient and multi-dimensional beings. These people of Terra are only left to wonder and to try to fathom and to grasp the concept of the knowledge, that these beings had procured concerning the knowledge of life and about the vastness of the universe that we are part of. The only way for those that are less fortunate is to delve into those ancient stories of those myths of the very ancient past. This is where one can learn about the knowledge of those ancient beings of those forgotten past ages of eons ago. Or for those that are fortunate, to meet with one or a few of these ancient beings that have been retuning and interacting with a select few of the people of Terra, to share their knowledge about life and what life is really about.

Why are only a select few chosen to have this interaction, you might ask? Those that are selected to have this interaction with some of these ancient beings are mainly the individuals that choose to have this contact with the ancient beings with no fear towards those that are from other star systems, regardless of what religions and government might create within the public about these beings.

A Journey into the Spiritual Quest of Who We Are: Book 4
The Quantum Leap into Consciousness

Where do these beings come from, you might also be asking?

These beings come from many star systems that are near our star and from within our galaxy and from distant galaxies from across the universe.

Below is a list of stars to name a few –

Lyra
Vega
Altair
Ophiuchus
Serpens
Centurus
Orion
Aldebaron
Eridanus
Arturus
Coma Berenices
Draco
Pleiades -there are several thousand star systems that make up the Pleiadean system. To name a few-
Atlas
Alcyone
Maia
Marope
Sy
Pleione
Asterope
Electra
Celanea

A Journey into the Spiritual Quest of Who We Are: Book 4
The Quantum Leap into Consciousness

Taygeta
Apsu - Terra (Earth) star

And many, many others star systems.

There are many other beings that are from many other systems, which are from other galaxies. Our galaxy is but one out of a trillion other galaxies that are in existence throughout this universe that we are in, and other universes that are beyond our comprehension.

On the next page, you will see where our sun is located within our group of stars and its surroundings within the vastness of this galaxy that we are part of.

You are looking at our Milky Way Galaxy at about 112 million light years away, and the location of our sun within the group of stars that we can see in our night sky. This is just one galaxy out of trillions of galaxies that makes up a universe.

Now you can have an idea on where our sun and our group of stars are located.

A Journey into the Spiritual Quest of Who We Are: Book 4
The Quantum Leap into Consciousness

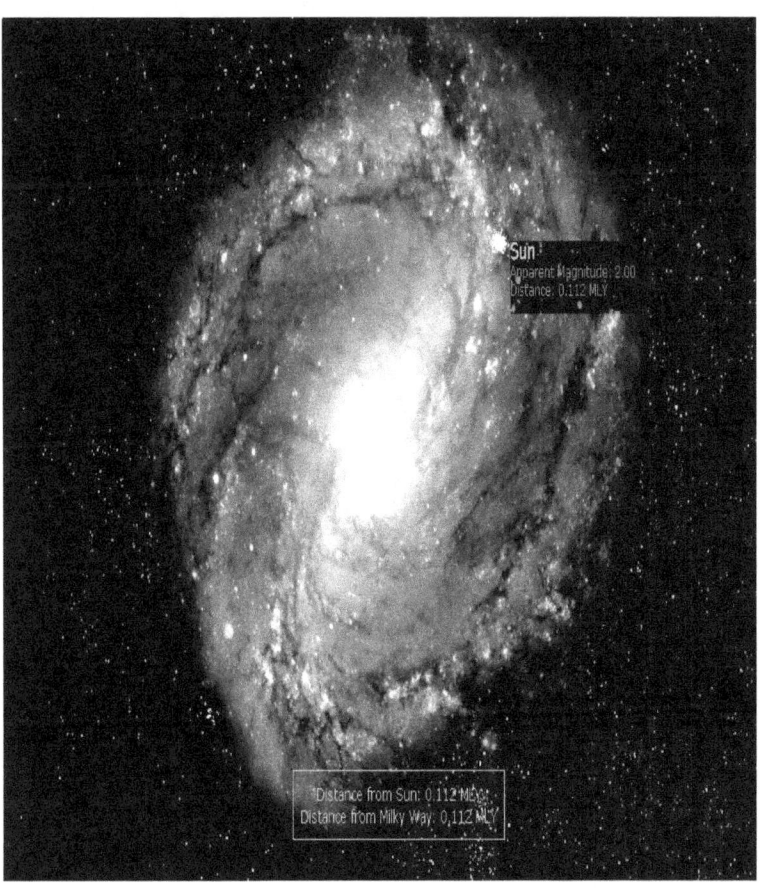

A Journey into the Spiritual Quest of Who We Are: Book 4
The Quantum Leap into Consciousness

Eunuch – Is a being that is of both genders.

The Eunuch was a being of both genders within itself. These beings existed upon the earth up until the last completion of the cycle that our group of stars made around our galaxy, which was around twelve thousand years ago. This was their end on the earth due to the energies that the earth was going through. These beings existed on Terra from about two-hundred thousand years ago up to twelve thousand years ago.

There are many pre ancient stories of these beings that were of both male and female gender. You just have to know how to translate those stories.

A Journey into the Spiritual Quest of Who We Are: Book 4
The Quantum Leap into Consciousness

On the continent of Tampaurban, they have those ancient stories of these beings that existed before twelve thousand years ago, and then shortly after this time these beings began to change and separate into individual male and female beings. From this change came forth a being of a new race, which is known as pre human race. These beings were a little bit different than the way we are today, they did not have the bellybutton as we do. Both of these beings lived for several hundreds to thousands of years. This story and many others are similar to the story of what people are reading about in the stories within the so-called bible, of a humanoid race of beings that was of both genders. This one being separated into another race of beings that brought forth a new race that is known as the pre -human race, and from this race of beings came the human race of today.

A Journey into the Spiritual Quest of Who We Are: Book 4
The Quantum Leap into Consciousness

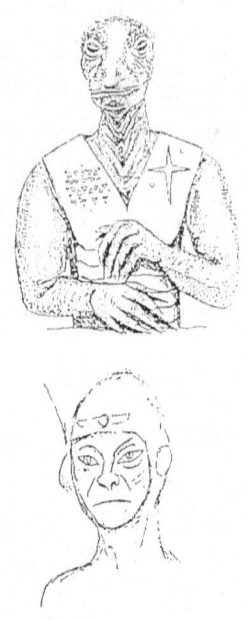

Top picture is one type of a Reptilian race.
Bottom picture is of a Serpent race.

Both of these beings, Reptilian and Serpent played parts within all stories of our pre-ancient myths and the stories within the bible and right up to the stories of today.

These beings have been around for well over three-hundred thousand years and they come from many star systems around our galaxy. For the Reptilian beings, a few of them come from the Sirius Star system, some are from the Orion star system, and some come from the star system of

A Journey into the Spiritual Quest of Who We Are: Book 4
The Quantum Leap into Consciousness

Draco. For the Serpent Beings a few of them are from the star system of Ophiuchus and many other systems throughout our galaxy and other galaxies as well.

The top and bottom pictures are ideas of types of hybrids of human and humanoid beings, along with the beings that are known as the greys.

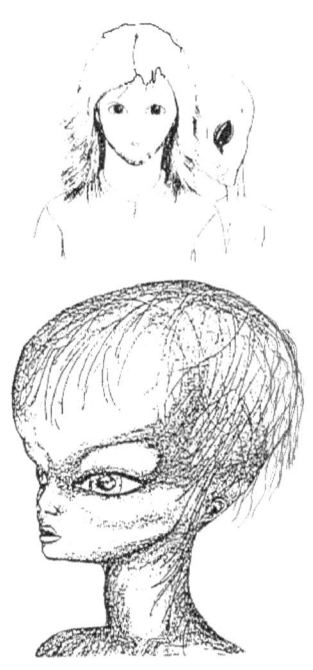

A Journey into the Spiritual Quest of Who We Are: Book 4
The Quantum Leap into Consciousness

These types of hybrid beings are of the next generation of beings, which are a combination of several genetics of DNA strands from many species from across the universes, which also includes our human DNA. We are just beginning to hear about these beings in our day in age. As we enter into our new cycle, our new age, we will be seeing more of these beings, but not until we can accept and get along with all the beings that are part of our old world. This is in the process of happening at this time, (the human race), so maybe in about another twenty plus years we might meet these hybrid beings that will be a new race of beings on this world.

A Journey into the Spiritual Quest of Who We Are: Book 4
The Quantum Leap into Consciousness

The drawings of the typical, Yeti, Bigfoot Also known as the Lemurian Beings.

A Journey into the Spiritual Quest of Who We Are: Book 4
The Quantum Leap into Consciousness

These ancient races of beings are the survivors of an ancient race from Lemuria. These beings existed for over two-hundred thousand years. They are widely read about in pre-ancient myth. They are also known throughout our current culture, but you call them by many names based on their locations around the world today. You call them the Yeti, Bigfoot, and many other names. These beings moved into their quantum leap into consciousness around twenty-five thousand years ago and they are multi-dimensional beings, they exists in our world around us, and also in the sixth dimensional world. These beings have telepathic ability for communication to those that are able to communicate telepathically. They come into our dimension at times, to check up on us in a way of speaking that is, since we too are moving from our 3rd dimensional existence and entering into the 4th and 5th dimensional existence. We will be seeing more of these beings in the near future.

One might ask, why are these beings of these other star systems interested in us, and why have they been watching over our star system and planet?

The one reason is that we are their brothers and sisters. We are on this earth as many forms of species, not all life is based on the human species. Most people cannot come to believe that there is other life besides ours in this galaxy, that there are other beings that exist on Terra. All you have to do is look around you; there are other species of life

A Journey into the Spiritual Quest of Who We Are: Book 4
The Quantum Leap into Consciousness

besides humans. There are other life forms which are more intelligent that the human species is, a thousand times more. This is mainly because these species are thousands of years older than our current human species is. The other reason for the return of some ancient beings back to our star system is that our star system is moving into a new age, a new cycle of life, and a new frequency of energy. I talked about that from the very beginning with Book 1, The Reawakening, and throughout this whole series. Yes everything and everyone is moving forward on the ladder of evolution on consciousness. Some and I mean only a hand-full have already moved forward into this consciousness of reawakening and they are beginning to awaken to the realization of who they are as conscious beings. Some of these star beings are here on our request and some of the other beings are here to observe the transition of all species that are on the earth as we all enter into our new beginning of this new cycle of life. As we reawaken that knowledge that lies within all of us, we come to the realization and the understanding of who we are as conscious beings. These beings from the stars are paving the way in front of all of us, they are the way showers, they ask for those beings that are on this world that had already reawakened to assist them in helping the rest of the beings on Terra that had not yet awakened.

A Journey into the Spiritual Quest of Who We Are: Book 4
The Quantum Leap into Consciousness

These ancient beings that were on our world several thousands of years ago are returning to Terra system, from those far off stars that these beings are coming from. As all of you might recall in those ancient stories, which are part of our mythology stories as you call them. All those beings had always been interacting with this star system for millions of years, and will continue to do so when the beings of this star system request their interactions. Or these star beings will take it upon themselves to interact with the inhabitants of a planet based on the changes of the cycle, energy frequency that a star system is entering into. Or if a being is needed to be placed on the planet to help influence the people to change before the new cycle begins. But for us at this new age, that we are entering which began as of the year 2000 which was paved before us two-thousand years ago, on that reawakening of who we truly are. It has taken this long, but that was only due to our past age that ended back in 1985.

The galaxy that we are in is finally moving forward into a new beginning, a new age, this also goes for all beings that are within this galaxy. We all are leaving the past age, that old energy and moving into a very new frequency. This is also why there is interest in these stars systems and all the beings in this sector of this galaxy. This is to observe all life and to see if they are reawakening and realizing, who they are, as conscious beings and to see if they are ready to move and to take that quantum leap into

A Journey into the Spiritual Quest of Who We Are: Book 4
The Quantum Leap into Consciousness

consciousness. As I said earlier only a hand full had already came to the understanding of who they are as conscious beings. Those that have already reawakened are not controlled by the so-called god theory of those religions. This hand full is about 5 % plus of the human species and that is pretty small hand full to say the least. This is why the awakened beings upon your planet called for assistance in paving the way, to help all beings on your planet realize who each and every one of you are. That way you can become aware of who you are and take that next step of evolution!

A Journey into the Spiritual Quest of Who We Are: Book 4
The Quantum Leap into Consciousness

Chapter 6

Entering the Halls of Cosmic Creations

Once again, we come to the realization of who we are as the conscious beings that we are, and that we create all that is around us and beyond us.

A Journey into the Spiritual Quest of Who We Are: Book 4
The Quantum Leap into Consciousness

As we look at the picture on the opposite page, we can see an idea of the halls of cosmic creations. We can see corridors upon corridors and within these corridors are archways. Each of these archways are cosmic creations. Each of these archways are what you might call the void, since these archways are void of creation. They are void until someone enters into the archway and they create their creation within this archway. Also remember that other beings also enter into these archways. Does that mean they will experience what was created before them? Not necessarily. Other beings enter these archways and they create their own creation within that archway as well, so then this archway starts to fill up with many ideas of creations.

Even in an archway that might appear to be void of creation is a creation within itself. Maybe the being that is within this void had created this void for one's own experience of nothingness, the emptiness of no thought, but it is still a creation, it is the stillness of creation. In addition as one enters into this archway they bring with them their own creation. Does this mean that the void is changed? No. Does this mean that the one that enters the void will experience the void? No. However, they will cross the path of each other's creation, somewhere along their paths of creation.

A Journey into the Spiritual Quest of Who We Are: Book 4
The Quantum Leap into Consciousness

Why there are so many ideas of creations within each archway, when there are many archways within the halls of cosmic creations, you might ask?

The reason is basically that there are many beings within that path of that particular cosmic birth and all exist within each other's creations and all are crossing into each other's path of creation.

Well why can you not have one creation per archway, so to say?

That would be like putting yourself in a room with no one else in there with you. This will give you that one creation to experience and nothing else. I think you will also go crazy, for there will be no one else to cross your path, no one for you to be part of their creation and for them to be part of your creation. The creation of only one creation within itself will be a boring place and very limited as well, since there can only be one being within that creation. Because as soon as you have two beings within a single creation, it no longer exists as a single creation, it now becomes a multiple creation. Now do you see and understand about the concepts of creations?

This is the knowledge that we are all reawakening within ourselves, the knowledge of becoming those conscious beings that we are, finally realizing who we are.

This is transpiring on Terra and within your entire Milky Way Galaxy. All beings that are within these universes are moving forward in consciousness and all beings are reawakening the knowledge within themselves and accepting that each of us are our own creator of our own creation. And through this acknowledgement and acceptance, we are finally able to take responsibility for our creations, which are amongst the many other creations which are around all of us at all times.

In addition, we are now ready to interact with other beings creations, which were created by other conscious beings, which exist in the universes that are around us.

How are we going to be able to interact with these other creations and those other beings of consciousness, you might ask?

Not any different from the way you interact with all the beings that are on your world. This is why there are so many species on your world. Yes the human beings are a species as well. As all of you are moving into becoming conscious beings, all the fears towards each other of controlling the other will all disappear in time. In addition, you will no longer be part of that experience of life and at the same time, you all will get along with the other species that are amongst your world. At that time all of you will be able to accept all the other life that exists amongst the stars, which has been amongst all of you as well.

What do these other beings look like?

A Journey into the Spiritual Quest of Who We Are: Book 4
The Quantum Leap into Consciousness

We showed you these other beings throughout the whole series and within this book. There are millions upon millions of many types of beings that exist throughout all the universes. The beings that we have been encountering within our time have been showing a curiosity about our species (the human race) and all beings that are upon Terra, and our technologies that we been developing for the past 2-3 hundred years. At the same time watching us on how we use this technology, on ourselves, (the human race) and watching us battling each other for no reason other than to see how one can kill another being of the same race. The beings are watching us from above the earth as we go about destroying the world that we all exist upon. As if we have no concern for Terra as the 'conscious living being', that she is, and seeing that we show no respect to our world and to all types of beings that are upon her. Beings are coming to our star system from all corners of our galaxy to see what is going on, on this unique planet which has millions of different beings upon it, to see how all these beings exist together. But we do not exist together! Not even with our own species (the human race)! One time in the ancient past ages we all existed together and respected all beings that were on our world, and including beings that are off our world. However, in the past current age we lost that connection.

A Journey into the Spiritual Quest of Who We Are: Book 4
The Quantum Leap into Consciousness

As we enter into our new age in the year 2,000 C.E (Current Era), we will start to see this respect towards other beings on this planet and the respect towards our own species; we will begin to come together as one race. We will be stopping this so called separating of the human race, which was created to separate the other continents, or due to belief systems. All this is changing right before your eyes. In addition, as we make this change towards all these beings, and that includes us the human beings, we will be able to show the same respect towards those beings, which are our brothers and sisters, which travels through the stars.

Do you want these beings of the stars to show respect towards you, when you are out amongst the stars?

I hope so!

Because I know, I would want that for myself!

What might exist within those other creations that are created by other beings that we might come to experience as we cross into their paths?

What one will come to experience within any given creation is solely up to one's own thoughts. Remember any and all creations are nothing more than the mere thought which later becomes, the basis for a creation to be experienced, if it would be in the future of the present or if it be the future of a distant future. It is not any different than let's say, how many thoughts you can have on how you want your life to be, or your future to be. You are creating all of those thoughts during your existence here on Terra and off Terra, as one day when you are alive or even after you had left this life on Terra. You are creating all those existences to experience, that even goes for the people that are creating those places that religious people are creating of their so called heaven, hell, purgatory even the void or whatever (which people still call it heaven). It is not called heaven it is called the universes, and yes, there are other types of beings that exists amongst the stars, there are many conscious beings that do exists out there, as I have shown you throughout this series.

In addition, there is no being that is called god or the devil. It is time that all of you face the facts that was all an illusion that was created as a veil to keep you from learning of the truth about this knowledge of who you are.

All the creations that you see around you, we created this in our past, to go about experiencing it in the future, which is now the present.

With these creations, that we all are experiencing exists many worlds within our own world.

Like-minded people through all the universes have said it, repeatedly. "A door way to ones dreams is another ones door way to his reality!"

Within this part, I am going to give you insight to these doorways or gateways to other dimensions and universes that are in existence in this world and beyond.

A Journey into the Spiritual Quest of Who We Are: Book 4
The Quantum Leap into Consciousness

These gateways come in many different shapes and in different locations around the world. Just to name a couple, the great pyramid of Giza, The Bermuda Triangle, Stonehenge and Sedona along with the Japanese Triangle along with many others.

Now the gateways I just listed above are on a large-scale size. Within these gateways which are all around the world, are energy levels that are able to get so intense at times, that strange phenomenal events occur within these gateways boundaries that can transport you to other dimensions. The energy level could also transport you to a universe many hundreds of millions of light years away, or it could send you several hundred of light years away from where you are now, or they could even send you to another dimension within this earth.

Let's now take a look at these gateways energies, what they are capable of doing to our energy when these gateways are operating at their minimal power when we step into their boundaries. First, we will look at the pyramid of Giza. The energy within this pyramid is capable of raising the physical energy of the body to another level of existence of awareness of our spiritual being. The awakening I am mentioning here is the awakening of the soul or spirit energy of our true essence of who we truly are. This is the question that everyone seems to wonder to themselves, time and time again "Who am I, and why have we come to this planet, what must we do while we are here?" Anyone entering the pyramid will go through this energy transformation process, there is no need to worry, it will not hurt you, because this transformation is harmless in all ways you can imagine. Through this transformation, it only changes the energy patterns within each individual being. This energy is to awaken the soul, so the body and soul can better communicate with each other and with the other universal beings that exist in the universes that are all around us. However, not everyone needs to go through this way of awakening of the soul's energy within all of us.

The second gateway is the Bermuda Triangle in the Atlantic Ocean. What is it with the Bermuda Triangle that has people all over this world in fear or in curiosity of this place? Could the fears be brought upon by all the disappearance of ships, planes, boats, and divers, along with other strange phenomenal events dating as far back to 1500's and even farther. Could this curiosity be brought forth by early spotted pyramid structures of a continent called Atlantis that has started rising from its twelve thousand-year watery grave? Or shall I say started to be uncovered by the movement of the sandy ocean bottom, by the shifting waters over onto other landmasses to cover them up, in order to reveal this old and ancient land. Here is another idea why people fear this place; it is because people do not know what is waiting to be revealed to them. On the other hand, is this curiosity of finding the truth about our universal origins, our true spot in the universes

A Journey into the Spiritual Quest of Who We Are: Book 4
The Quantum Leap into Consciousness

around us? What happens when a person or anything entering the boundaries of the Bermuda Triangle when the energy is at its highest in certain areas? Some might say those people are lost forever, those people that say that are wrong, these people are merely transported to another dimension within this world, or they are transported to another universe that lies beyond our comprehension of reality.

To find the true answers of the Bermuda Triangle, there are three places to find the answers.

The first place is in the minds of the people of today that lived during the time of Atlantis.

The second is in the minds of the people that were transported out to another dimension or to other universes that are beyond this dimension and universe, which might have returned back to this reality.

The last place that you may find the answers is in the minds of the Star Travelers that have visited the earth for the past ninety five thousand years.

As I mentioned earlier, you can be transported to another dimension on this planet. Let me take this moment to explain to you about this transportation. Within this form of teleportation to another dimension within this planet, you would need two doorways existing simultaneously. They do not need to be in the same location, and the second doorway can be activated at a different time and a different dimension as well. When the first doorway or gateway is opened and you step into this gateway, you pass into space where time does not exist. You then pass into the second gateway, upon it opening, you will find yourself in an alternate dimension that you were not part of to start with. In addition, you will find your physical appearance not any different from when you entered the first gateway even if it has been, say, one hundred years from when you first stepped into the first gateway. The reason that you do not age is because that you are traveling in space where time has no effect upon you at all. However, when you step through the other end, time will start again for you, unless you step through a gateway that does not have time in its existence.

I also presented to you within book 1 The Reawakening, about the cycles that the earth has been through over the past several ages, of the changing of the energies and of other dimensions that the earth has gone through.

So why all the need for all this thought of all these creations, which are all around us, with all types of beings?

At this particular point as we are entering into our new age, we are moving from the 3rd dimensional existence and going into the 4th and 5th dimensional existence, this is why we are seeing these other beings within our dimension. It is because all dimensions are moving forward to the next dimension, so this brings all dimensions to a point of crossing within each other's dimensions which are next to each other, such as a creation

A Journey into the Spiritual Quest of Who We Are: Book 4
The Quantum Leap into Consciousness

moves into the existence of the 1st dimension, the 1st dimension moves into the 2nd dimension, the 2nd dimension moves into the 3rd dimension (ours), the 3rd dimension (ours) moves into the 4th and the 5th dimension simultaneously, and the 4th and 5th dimensions move into the 6th dimension and so on and so forth. So at times, there might be several dimensions existing together at the same time.

All of these creations are unique onto themselves because we are unique conscious beings onto ourselves, because no two thoughts of our own are the same, all of our thoughts are also different from another person's thoughts, and no two people's thoughts are the same. So, this brings forth the many thoughts of forms and types of creations that might exist, for all forms and types of beings to experience within all these creations from lifetime to lifetime, the endlessness of all the forms of creation to experience and not have any two the same. This is why we are seeing this interaction of other beings from all corners of all the universes coming to this unique place in space, to our planet, because there are millions of beings on Terra creating millions of types of creations within a section of a galaxy which we are in. These beings are of many origins from across all the universes that are coming to this sector of this universe. These beings are coming to this sector of our galaxy to experience other forms of creations, other dimensions of experiences other than theirs to interact with, other paths of creation which are created by other forms of conscious beings of other creations which are created by other forms of conscious beings of other creations and other thoughts. We started to enter a new age, a new cycle of energy, and a new birth in the cosmic creation of worlds within worlds. Our world is evolving and growing and it is moving into another experience in the endlessness of experiences of experiencing other existences. All this is part of the cosmic creation of creations, not by any one being, but by all beings that exist in the vastness of all the universes that are around us at all times.

The Unseen World

I have been asked by Cindy (my wife) to share with all of you an experience that she had back in the spring of 1993. This is in the memory of Cindy, she moved onto her next existence on July 2, 1993. She had a lot to offer as a teacher of our spiritual understanding of the aspects of our existence, and upon her request, I am putting this information in this book.
~ Sometimes, it is very difficult to believe in something that you want when it has not manifested physically in your life. We are trained to believe in something only when it is physically before our eyes. This only destroys the trust that we need to have in ourselves. Every person is totally

responsible for everything in his and her lives. This does include everything good and bad. When we fail to acknowledge this, we look to someone or something else to blame for the mess in our lives.

At the center of the universe, energy creates everyone and everything. It appears as a light gray mist, and it molds itself to every thought we have and everything we say. The universal energy never doubts us, it just is. It automatically gives us what we want. The problem is that we are not prepared to receive what we want. It may be that whatever you are asking for is not for your highest good. On the other hand, maybe you do not believe that you have the power to create and have anything. The universe cannot give us what we deny ourselves.

You can start building trust in the universe and that, which has not physically manifested. First, you must build a solid trust in yourself. Trust in your ability to create what you want. Experiment with creating little things in your life first. Then you can move on and create bigger and better things.

Then you can trust the universe to supply you with everything you ask for. All you need to do is send the thought of what you want out and then release it. Then be patient for the universe to bring you what you want. Some things will take longer to come than others. It depends on what you want, how much you believe you deserve to have what you want. You can only live, build the trust in yourself and the universe one day at a time. Please do not be discouraged if it takes some time to receive what you ask for. If you really want something, never give up.

We all come here to earth to learn our lessons and fulfill our desires. One important lesson to learn is that we are all one. The hate and violence must end sometime. The sooner we all recognize that there is no separation between us and if we all love each other unconditionally, then the violence will end.

The negativity on your planet is reaching its maximum level. The energy will be shifting to positive and we will have one thousand plus years of peace. This is called the Age of Aquarius. This planet Terra so desperately needs love and peace. All of us here on earth deserve to have our desires fulfilled, and live in a world of love and peace. ~

Chapter 7

The Arrival of New Guardians

It was many ages ago, to be exact it was one cycle ago, when your sun traveled around the galaxy and completed that cycle. Imagine your galaxy divided into thirteen parts and which your sun (star) within its group of stars moves through these parts through time. And imagine your galaxy doing the same thing moving through the thirteen parts of your universe, through time as well, it would be like a wheel within a wheel, with each wheel having thirteen parts, one time around your galaxy through these thirteen parts or ages as they are known as it makes the completion of one cycle around your galaxy. See diagram below.

Our group of stars rotating around one another, and rotating around the galaxy at the same time:

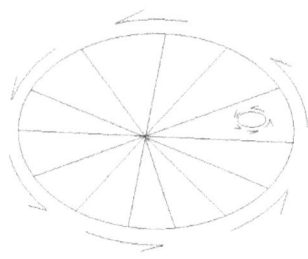

A Journey into the Spiritual Quest of Who We Are: Book 4
The Quantum Leap into Consciousness

Everything rotates within and around itself like hands on a clock.

This process brings in a new age or cycle, it all depends on what our group of stars are in the process of going through and what our galaxy is going through within the universe that we are part of. Now you have a wheel, within a wheel, within a wheel, so on and so forth.

See diagram below.

Our universe that we all are in also rotates as well.

Other galaxies: The Milky Way galaxy

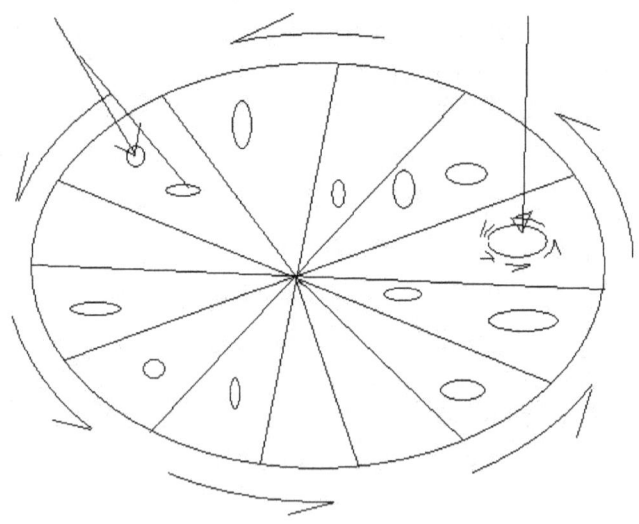

A Journey into the Spiritual Quest of Who We Are: Book 4
The Quantum Leap into Consciousness

As your galaxy is rotating within itself, it is also rotating through the universe along with millions of other galaxies as well, all rotating at different speeds.

It was a cycle ago that the Cetaceans became conscious beings and became the guardians of the knowledge of the universe and became the guardians of the earth, along with other conscious beings within this galaxy and amongst other galaxies around our universe. These beings are mentioned throughout our mythology stories of our planets past cycles.

All these ancient beings at one time or another also became conscious beings and started their reawakening of the knowledge of who they are as conscious beings and learning the knowledge of the universe. As these beings of the universe became conscious beings and came into our star system and seeing these beings of this earth was just beginning to become conscious beings themselves, (the Cetaceans). So those beings of the stars taught the Cetaceans the knowledge of who they are as conscious beings, and about the earth also as a conscious living being, and these star beings also taught the Cetaceans the knowledge of the universe, which we all are part of. As I mentioned in Book 3, the human species are not the guardians of the earth, but it is the Cetaceans that are the guardians of the earth and they hold the knowledge of the universe. Now your group of stars has completed another cycle around your galaxy. As you come to this completion, the human beings are arriving at their awakening of becoming the conscious beings that you are. You have arrived to the point of earning, of becoming conscious beings with the many, which are amongst the universe. This is where the new guardians of this new cycle, this new age will come from. These new guardians will receive the knowledge from the previous guardians, like the Cetaceans and the beings from other galaxies within our universe and from beyond. This is why all these ancient star traveling beings, have this interest in this sector of our galaxy. It is because of this new age that all of us are entering into at this time.

   There are millions of civilizations among our galaxy alone, that are moving forward, but not all at the same pace, but all and all, you are moving forward into becoming the conscious beings that you are. Even the human beings are moving up the ladder of evolution and becoming conscious beings as well, but not all of you are moving at the same pace. For those that have already became conscious being, that have taken that step of quantum leap into consciousness, you will have a chance of becoming the new guardians of Terra, among the Cetaceans and the other beings from the stars that have already became conscious beings, ages ago. Yes, a few humans have already taken that next step into consciousness. They are the new guardians of the

A Journey into the Spiritual Quest of Who We Are: Book 4
The Quantum Leap into Consciousness

knowledge of the universe and will become the guardians of Terra in this new age.

But, before anyone becomes guardians among the ranks of those other old ancient guardians of knowledge and of Terra, you all will go through a learning of the knowledge that the universe holds within itself, which is the true meaning of itself and about becoming this conscious being that we all are. This is the knowledge that I have been presenting throughout this whole series, but this is only the tip of the iceberg. After these beings, (if it be humans or beings of other star systems or the many other beings that I presented throughout this series) have become conscious beings and learned of the knowledge of the universe. Once they have fully understood the concept of life, and the concepts of creation which is created merely from all beings thoughts within all the universes of their own creation, for their own experience within the many creations of creations, as an experience of the many forms of life to take part in. Then and only then, those beings that had taken that next step, that quantum leap into consciousness of becoming conscious beings, will become the guardians of the knowledge of the universes. In addition, it is those beings that will become the guardians of this planet and of their star system that they are part of. It is these guardians that are the teachers of the knowledge of the universes, they will become the teachers of the civilizations of their world(s) and

A Journey into the Spiritual Quest of Who We Are: Book 4
The Quantum Leap into Consciousness

help those beings to accomplish what they have already started, which is taking that next step into consciousness and becoming who they are, as conscious beings that we all are.

Yes, there have been some of the ancient beings of the past ages ago that were playing those roles of these gods. They were trying to prevent the human species that is across the universe, from accomplishing their next step of going into consciousness, by any means they deemed necessary to stop those civilizations from learning of the truth.

The time has now come to an end for those ancient beings that was playing those roles as gods and devils, of ages ago that was preventing other beings in the universe, from taking their next step into consciousness and learning the knowledge of the universes and of who we are as conscious beings!

Civilizations across the universe were lured away from learning of the truth by those beings that were playing those roles as gods! Now these ancient beings of truth are coming to the earth once again to teach us the knowledge of life. We are now able to take our next step into consciousness, along with the many other beings that are in our galaxy and within the vast universe that we all are part of.

Chapter 8

Time Ends

Now your star system had once again made another completion of traveling around the galaxy and a new cycle begins. Also at the same time your group of stars is entering a new age as well as a new cycle. This is a very interesting time for all beings that exist among your group of stars and your galaxy.

The ancient beings that are the guardians of the universal knowledge of the energy life force are the highest universal beings that exist in the universes around us. The universal knowledge of those beings holds the key to the knowledge that is not comprehended beyond the physical minds of today. It is these guardians of the ancient knowledge of the essence of the life force, which is brought forth by the minds of the ancient beings of beings from the universes. These beings bring forth the knowledge of the essence of the energy of the life force for the beginning of a new cycle and the new age for all beings to fully be part of. This knowledge of the universes is rightfully yours to know and to fully understand who you are. These ancient beings that brought this universal knowledge to you are not to be looked upon as gods, or your creators, or as devils, because they are not.

They were never meant to have these titles. It was the religions of Terra from around six to ten thousand years ago, that gave these non-meaning titles to these beings to bring fear into the people of the world. These ancient beings were simply known as the ancient beings of beings that are of many races from across the universes, because those ancient beings are known as the guardians, because of their superiority of the knowledge of the universes.

All of you on earth and all beings within this galaxy no matter what dimension you are in, are about to have this reawakening of this knowledge of who you are, as conscious beings as all of you take this quantum leap into consciousness, it brings with it great discipline and long training comes with, becoming a being of the knowledge of the universal energy. There is one thing that all beings and especially, "the human species," should start realizing, which is that every single being within this universe are all creators of their own creation that is all around you, along with taking the responsibility of the knowledge of the universe, which they hold within themselves. This is what I have been presenting to you throughout this whole series. This is the knowledge that all religions around the world have been hiding from all of you and getting you to believe in their way as their gods wanted you to believe in. Now you are finally able to see the truth that they, "your religions" been keeping you from.

There are a few things that hold a bond to you. In addition, you must rid yourself of those physical limitations of this physical plane, which are society's way of life. Religions and probably the most important one is, time. See, time does not exist anywhere except in your physical realm on Terra. Time is a human creation and used to measure how long it takes something to happen. They desperately want something to happen in a period, and when it does not happen by that time, they get frustrated and say it will never happen. With these limitations, it hinders the spiritual growth of one's evolution to the higher awareness in the universal knowledge of truth and wisdom. This is what this new cycle and this new age that we all are entering into is about, we are becoming conscious beings as we reawaken that ancient knowledge of the universes that lies waiting for us within ourselves.

A Meeting with the Being of Beings

I mentioned to the being of beings, "It is Time…"

The ancient being answered, "Indeed."

A Journey into the Spiritual Quest of Who We Are: Book 4
The Quantum Leap into Consciousness

I asked the being, "Show me who I am, reawaken all the knowledge within and bring it forth..."

Then the ancient being of beings asked, "Are you ready to unlock the knowledge of the universes within yourself?"

Yes, I am ready! I replied. After these past thirty seven years of learning, bring forth the knowledge of the past from the future to the present!

The ancient being was to the point. "You are the knowledge of the past from the future to the present! You are the past from the future to the present."

"What is the past – the future – and the present?" Asked the ancient beings of beings.

I replied to the being standing next to me, "Nothing more than, the now!"

The being said in a straightforward voice, "You are the beginning and the end, then the beginning again."

The ancient being of beings then asked me, "Tell me about time."

I replied to the ancient being of beings,
"Time bends...
Time folds...
Time is space...
Time ends..."

Then the ancient being asked, "What does all this mean?"

I answered, "We are everything that life is... life is everything that we are."

"We are the creators of what is all around us that are seen and unseen, along with us!"

The ancient being said in a satisfied voice, "Very good, you are now a guardian amongst the many which hold the true knowledge of the essence of the universes, which is within yourself!"

As we now come to realize, we all are our own Brahmas, creators, and we are the breath of our own creation, which we have created from our own experiences to experience within. This is the knowledge that those ancient beings of beings of ages long ago were trying to teach to us. We are now at our new cycle and our new age that is starting again. This time we are able to learn of the ancient knowledge that is coming forth again, for all to learn of the truth, without the interfering of those particular beings that were playing the roles as your gods and devils. These beings did not want you to learn of the knowledge of the universes and about who we are as conscious beings!

A Message
From the Ancient Beings of Beings

We were once where you are now, in the understanding of who we are as conscious beings!

You too will be where we are now, in the understanding of who you are!

A Journey into the Spiritual Quest of Who We Are: Book 4
The Quantum Leap into Consciousness

We were once like you, before we consciously evolved to who we are now!

The moment has come for you to, to become as we are now!

As other beings that are below you, will become as you were in the past!

We too will become as beings that are before us. So on and so forth!

The moment has finally arrived for all to claim your rite of passage to the knowledge of who you really are, and to take your place among the countless other beings that are before you, which are also amongst other conscious beings that are among all the universes seen and unseen. Stand up and take this step in the quantum leap into consciousness, which is rightfully yours and learn the true knowledge of life. End the way of letting beings control you and keep you in the dark (asleep). The more you become awakened and learn of the truth, these beings that are controlling you, will no longer be able to. At the same time, these beings that have been controlling you and bringing their ways of life to Terra, and having you kill each other and, having you divided on this earth will no longer be supported in this way of life any longer.

This next cycle and your new age are all about an end to the previous age of control. It is the moment to reawaken and become conscious beings and take responsibility for your thoughts and of what your thoughts create. It is up to each and every-one of you to take responsibility for your own thoughts and of what you are creating around you.

I want everyone to take a moment and really focus on these questions.

Do you want to continue living the way you have been for the past cycle, going around killing other human beings because your government says you must. Because your government says, those people are the ones that you must fear, so you must kill them?

Do you want to continue living your life with a religious belief system that tells you that you must believe a certain way based on a god that nobody has seen in over three thousand years? That (he or she) will come to earth and destroy you, or tell you are not worthy by gods standards?

Or do you want all of that to end and be able to live in peace and harmony with each other?

This is what your governments and your religious figures do not want! They do not want peace and harmony, mainly because they would not be able to create fear within you and they would not be able to control you either!

It is up to you to live in peace and harmony, to exist on this world and extend it into our group of stars and into our whole galaxy.

This is the choice that all of you have to make, at this point.

A Journey into the Spiritual Quest of Who We Are: Book 4
The Quantum Leap into Consciousness

Do you want to continue living in a world of control, fear, chaos and killing, all because someone says so?

On the other hand, do you want to live in a world of peace and harmony, the way it is meant to be?

What are you waiting for; decide now how you want to live your life on this earth!

That choice is totally up to each and every-one of you to decide on what you want no one can take that away from you!

If you had decided for peace, harmony, I would like you to send your voice out to the universe now, and say…

I want all this control, fear and killing all to stop, NOW!

I want peace and harmony on the earth and within our star group and within all the galaxies that make up our universes, seen and unseen. I want this right now!

This brings you to your next step on the evolution ladder and it takes you to the quantum Leap into consciousness.

I hope with the knowledge that I have presented to you throughout this series, that you have a better idea of what your life is truly is about. I hope this helps to remove the veils of illusions that kept all of you from learning the true knowledge of who you really are. If you start your reawakening and start to remove those veils of illusion, after reading these books, then I have accomplished what I set out to do. This is just the beginning of your reawakening of the knowledge of life and of learning of who we all are as conscious beings! Remember as you begin to awaken that there are others that have not reawakened yet, and it is up to those that have awaken to be teachers to those below you. Teach them what you have already learned, so they too can know what you know.

The knowledge of life is there for all to learn about and it is not for the select few. No one being has the right to tell you not to learn the true knowledge of life, and of who we all are. We are conscious beings and this knowledge is there for all!

What has been presented to you, within this series is the true knowledge of life. This is the knowledge that has been kept from by beings that did not want to evolve as they did, because they wanted other beings to control you. This is not going to go any longer, it stops here now!

> This is not the beginning of the end…
> It is also not the end…
> It is a new beginning…

A Journey into the Spiritual Quest of Who We Are: Book 4
The Quantum Leap into Consciousness

To be continued...

I leave you with a glimpse of the next book called –
- The Ancient Beings Who Are Among Us -
Coming in March 2008
ISBN 13: 978-0-9767832-6-8

A Journey into the Spiritual Quest of Who We Are: Book 4
The Quantum Leap into Consciousness

The Gathering

Within one world of many creations, we see a Terra type planet and on a mountain range, we see a larger pyramid city with many towers, temples and many pyramids that surround one very large pyramid that is about a mile tall that is located within the center of the city. On top of this large pyramid is a triple golden flame that has one flame in the middle and two flames going around the middle flame, and all three flames extend about fifty feet into the sky. Within this pyramid is a chamber where the ancient beings of beings meet. This chamber that the ancient beings meet is a circular room with a half sphere ceiling with a circular opening on top.

Within this chamber we see about one hundred beings wearing robes that cover them totally. The robes are multiple shades of gold and yellow with tints of shades of brown. These beings are gathered in this chamber conversing about a change, and we hear several voices male/female talking amongst themselves. There is a male being that is about six to seven feet tall standing in the middle of the chamber of the open floor, while the other beings are seated

A Journey into the Spiritual Quest of Who We Are: Book 4
The Quantum Leap into Consciousness

in chairs that face the open floor in this circular chamber. The being that is standing begins talking and mentions to the other beings… "Now… their journey begins… they are on their way, of beginning to be reawakened!"

We then hear a female voice from one of the beings that is seated in the circle… "We hope they reawaken before it becomes to late…" A male voice is heard from amongst the beings, "Do we need to give our assistance…?" The being that is standing in the middle of the room, turns to male being that asked the question, "Those that are already reawakening are coming together and helping those, which have not reawakened yet, to their conscious understanding of who they are as conscious beings." I am doing all that I can do to help those beings that are below us, in letting them know that the time has arrived to reawaken their knowledge of who they really are as conscious beings. It is a slow process since their knowledge has been asleep for the past six to ten thousand years. An additional assistance of the other beings may be required very shortly…"

A female voice is heard. "We are ready when you feel the need of our assistance to help awaken the other ancient beings of beings that are among those beings that are waiting to be reawaken…" Another female voice is heard. "We will begin to call those ancient beings here, and we will have them here for you, and they will be able to assist you when you need them to help on the reawakening process of these beings of the earth planet." The being that is standing in the middle of the chamber mentions, "I will monitor the earth civilizations journey and their reawakening, and I will let you know when the assistance of the other ancient beings are needed, for the reawakening of the civilization on earth."

The being that is standing in the middle of the chamber turns back into his original state of existence of a golden ball of energy, and leaves through the top of the chamber and goes through the triple golden flame that is at the top of this pyramid and disappears into the space above. Then soon after that, the other beings that are in the chamber leave the pyramid in their original state as well but of various colors. In addition, these beings also disappear into the space above the planet.

A Journey into the Spiritual Quest of Who We Are: Book 4
The Quantum Leap into Consciousness

A Journey into the Spiritual Quest of Who We Are: Book 4
The Quantum Leap into Consciousness

A Journey into the Spiritual Quest of Who We Are: Book 4
The Quantum Leap into Consciousness

A Journey into the Spiritual Quest of Who We Are: Book 4
The Quantum Leap into Consciousness

A Journey into the Spiritual Quest of Who We Are: Book 4
The Quantum Leap into Consciousness

A Journey into the Spiritual Quest of Who We Are: Book 4
The Quantum Leap into Consciousness

A Journey into the Spiritual Quest of Who We Are: Book 4
The Quantum Leap into Consciousness

www.ingramcontent.com/pod-product-compliance
Lightning Source LLC
Chambersburg PA
CBHW051451290426
44109CB00016B/1709